Life in a Desert

by Maryellen Gregoire

Nancy E. Harris, M.Ed—Reading
National Reading Consultant

capstone classroom

Heinemann Raintree • Red Brick Learning
division of Capstone

A cactus lives
in the desert.

A rabbit lives
in the desert.

A snake lives in the desert.

A bird lives
in the desert.

A lizard lives
in the desert.

A squirrel lives
in the desert.

A tarantula lives in the desert.

A skunk lives in the desert. Look out!